Still Crazy After All These Quilts

By Charlotte Angotti

Preface

When I first began thinking about writing a book, one of my students and a good friend, Mary Margaret Pariser, was taking a class from me. She asked me when was I writing a book. I answered with a question, "on quilting or my life?" And she replied, straight faced, "Charlotte, any book you write will have a whole lot of life in it!"

So, with that thought, I have tried to give this book a breath of life that will inspire and motivate you to quilt and create.

This book is for all the students, friends and family that know just how crazy my life can be and still love me just the same.

A special thanks goes to the people that stuck by me at my most crazy times; Michael, Jo Ann, Steve, Nancy, my family, and all my students for their undying belief that this book was possible. And to David Hopkins for giving me this opportunity. Last, but never forgotten, a real big hug to Mary Ellen Hopkins, the queen of crazy ladies everywhere. May I please walk in your shadow? I never stop learning from your endless supply of shortcuts and better ways of taking the difficult and making it simple.

This book is for quilters everywhere. Quilting is just like life, learn to take the difficult and make it look simple.

Table Of Contents

All quilts in this book made by Charlotte Angotti except Min's 1950 quilt.

Author can be contacted at;
1002 Hanson Way
Virginia Beach, VA 23454

ISBN 0-929950-15-1

ME PUBLICATIONS
1604 SANTA MONICA BLVD.
SANTA MONICA, CA, 90404
Tel 800/527-2665   Fax 310/394-2458

Publisher
ME Publications
Author
Charlotte Angotti
Graphic Design
George Maimon
Photography
Michael Negly

Introduction

Just like everything in my life, this book will begin with a story because I love telling good stories.

One day when I got home from work, there was a package on my porch from my godmother, Min McElvy. I live in Virginia and she lived in Alabama. There wasn't a note or a card but inside that box, much to my surprise, there was a crazy quilt Min's mother made her in the 50s.

Of course I picked up the phone and called her to thank her and find out more about this treasure. I was familiar with crazy quilts, but not really interested, until that moment. It goes back to a saying I have always used, "I never met a quilt I didn't like if someone was giving it to me." There were flowers and lots of "things" on this heavy quilt. She told me her mother made it, and she was going through some things and wanted me to have the quilt. I told her how much I liked this crazy quilt, and that it would always be a treasure to me.

At that she snapped back, "Well, it's not real pretty and it's old, but you don't have to keep calling it crazy!"

Let me try to explain crazy quilting to you as I tried to explain it to Min. Way back in the old days, before 7-11 stores, when women had to prove their husbands provided them such a great life that they even had leisure time. This wasn't an easy thing to do with all those kids, a big house, no electricity, out door bathrooms, and oh, those clothes. But, she did needlework to show off her skills and prove her leisure time. The Victorian Age was when crazy quilting became the rage. By taking velvets, satins, and other beautiful fabrics left over from those clothes they wore, they sewed patches together. Then using their needlework skills, they would add embroidery stitches to cover every seam. The beauty of these quilts was in all the different embellishments, ribbons from the fairs, silks from cigars, flowers from hats – anything from their lives. They would display these works of art in the parlor for their guests to see. These quilts weren't very useful, – pretty heavy and difficult to clean – but they were, and still are, works of art. I never had much use for them until I got that package. Then I became interested.

I took a class from Judith Montano and learned lots of wonderful things about crazy quilting, including how to do those beautiful stitches, make ribbon roses, and all sorts of fancy stuff. Only thing was, I could never see myself making anything really useful.

That's the problem I had in art classes, too. I never really understood the "noodles glued to a paper plate" type of art that was taught to kids all over the USA.

But, I liked making the patchwork; it was fun. The problem was I had found "crazy" and no reason to do it. Being a quilter that loves to piece I thought it seemed logical to put the "crazy" together with my patchwork blocks. So, I came up with this crazy patchwork thing and I'm crazy about it!

So you will understand me a little better, let me say that I quilt because I love to. When it stops being fun, I'll quit. This is a hobby, yes it's also my job, too. Relax and enjoy quiltmaking and you will make better quilts. Don't feel you have to do it my way, exactly, or use the same colors I have. This is the beauty of quiltmaking—just like us, all quilts are different.

Projects that never get finished are not very good projects. Therefore, the projects in this book are geared for completion. Some of my quilting friends, especially Karen Schaller, say that when the top is finished so is the quilt. Hopefully, these projects will even make it to the quilted stage of finished Remember you're having fun.

The projects in this book are small and make great wall hangings. With lots of beads and fancy work, and by making them small, you can show them off by hanging them throughout your home. Those that have less embellishments could easily be made larger. Do not limit yourself.

The names of the patterns have been changed. The real names of the patterns, as I know them, are in ( ) in the title of each section. Understand that change is common in quiltmaking. That is one reason there are so many names of patterns already. One woman named a pattern and shared it with another woman. She changed it to fit her life and renamed it something she liked. I want to keep the original names familiar to everyone but also want to change them because the patterns have gone crazy.

Please let me know any new names you come up with because it lets me know you are working and thinking.

Charlotte Angotti

First Step is Just Getting Crazy

Some of you may know what "crazy" is but you may not be sure how to get it exactly. Here, let me say you should refer to Judith Montano's "Crazy Quilt Handbook" for more details on crazy quilting if you don't understand this method.

This method is fun and fast so don't spend any time worrying about grains or different fabrics. In crazy quilting there are no rules of sewing only guidelines that make it easier.

Begin with a square of muslin (or you can use that ugly 1978 fabric that you can't throw away, but know you will never use). This square needs to be larger than what your final center measurement will be. [Example: you need a final center measurement of 4 1/2". Cut a 6 1/2" square. Don't panic about waste! You can never get it back if it's too small, but you can always cut off what's too big. Have a base fabric for each block you are making.

Choose your fabrics for the center of the crazy patchwork. Usually 8 or 9 pieces is more than enough. The yardage you need to make the crazy is very small. Usually scraps work well. These do not have to be special fabrics–but can be. If you are using fancy fabrics, 1/8 yard pieces or fat quarters work well and you get more variety having more fabrics. Use cottons if that is the look you desire. Depending on how many squares you are making, usually less than a yard and one half total is needed for all your crazy squares. Usually my center fabric is a print with lots of colors, but this is not a law. Using your center fabric, cut enough five sided shapes to have one for each block (diagram #1).

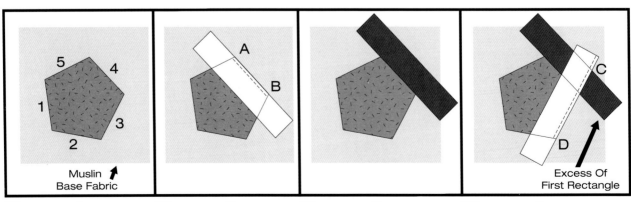

| Diagram 1 | Diagram 2 | Diagram 3 | Diagram 4 |

Take your other fabrics and cut some small rectangles. This makes the fabric easier to handle. Lay a rectangle along the longest edge of your center, right sides together. Sew from point A to point B (diagram #2). Do not cut any excess yet. Open and press (diagram #3). If you are right-handed go clockwise around the center 5-sided shape as in diagram #4. If you are left handed, go counterclockwise. After sewing C to D, the excess of the first rectangle can be cut away from underneath. Open and press.

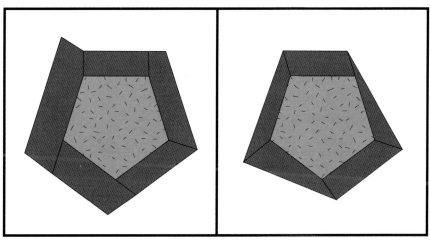

Diagram 5

Continue around the center until all sides of the center are covered. You can now cut these rectangles into different shapes instead of just rectangles. This will add more interest around the center. (diagram #5)

Continue to sew on and cut fabric rectangles as above until the square of base fabric is completely covered. Try to get a good variety of shapes, sizes, fabrics and textures if possible. After the crazy is sewn, trim the entire base to the size required for your block. The seams now need to be covered with some type of stitch or embellishment. I do most of this on my sewing machine and I use the decorative stitches. You remember those stitches you have never wanted, never really used and couldn't understand why they were on you machine–yeah, those stitches. There is something I should explain. My definition of higher learning isn't just college. I believe higher learning is taking something you know and adding something new and it suddenly gives you something greater, better, and hopefully more exciting, than if either of the two somethings were all alone. Just like I knew how to sew patchwork and I added crazy. It is something different. The decorative stitches on the sewing machine is another example–we know they are there and how to use them, now we have a great place to put them.

By using fancy threads you can really spice up a flat piece. There are those great threads you see in the quilt shops and wonder about. You may even have some for-whatever reason. Now is the time to use them. Sometimes these threads are difficult to use. A cone holder may help and a larger eye needle will help. A better quality metallic thread is easy to use and less likely to break. Every machine is different, one thread that works for one machine may not work as well for another. These threads come in many colors and really are fun to create with once you find the one that works for you. By adding these threads, buttons, charms, and other embellishments, you can create something magnificent. Each crazy square is now a little art masterpiece of its very own.

Let's talk about Fabrics & Yardages

Crazy uses very small amounts of fabrics. In fact you get a lot of crazy from very little substance. Whenever asked, "how much fabric do I buy," I remind people that I own a shop so I buy by the bolt. (Someone told me the story about a shop owner that died and had more bolts at home than in her shop. At that I asked, "does this mean she wins?") When I travel or go to shows I do buy from other shops and unless my funds are limited I never buy less than a yard. Everything less seems too small for anything but trouble. Usually I buy more than a yard, very rarely less.

The quilts I made for this book were made from my stash. A stash is where a fabric without a project goes to wait. You can get better quilts working from lots of fabrics. Fabrics you like and have bought simply because you liked it will make better quilts for you. You will be less limited because all the newest fabrics are still available to use, like the extra special one (or ten) on the shelf in your sewing area. For those that are just beginning to collect fabric or for you that think this is a silly way to sew, let me explain a stash. You will never stop collecting fabrics for a stash. As soon as you use some you need to replace it and your stash can always stand to have that extra splash of your favorite color.

To most quilters their stash is some secret, hidden, magical wonder of fabric they never plan to use so they buy very small pieces to have and to hold until death they-do-part. Some, I've heard say, are taking it with them. Others are telling their friends to hurry to their sewing rooms before "he" finds the stash they talk about after they die-like it matters about the stash! And newsflash, your friend won't be able to make anything wonderful either if all you are leaving her is small pieces to look at.

Your stash needs a new image if the above person is you, girls & boys! And something you must understand, your stash is your paint. Do you understand what that sentence really means? Your stash is your paint. When I took art, and oh, I have taken lots of art classes, the first day of any painting class you will get a list of colors you must have. Not maybe, or just some, but must have. These colors will be everything. They will be color, light and darkness and everything in between. They will blend and mix and do wonderful things. But you can't, won't, no way paint without them. Your fabrics, in your favorite colors, prints, shapes and yardages are your paints–you can't, won't, no way quilt without them.

So, next time someone asks you the famous question asked of everyone in a quilt shop, "what are you going to make with that fabric? Answer them, "paint a masterpiece." And you need lots of paint, so buy it.

When you begin getting a stash you need a place for it. Move the less important people out and take that room for yourself. (Notice how I'm working on your self image!) You are an artist, with an attitude. Usually we are the last person of importance in the world–get a number closer to the top, I'm sure you're worth it! Get yourself some space in that place you take care of so well and call it your very own. Get some shelves so you can store your fabrics. You need to see them and they need to breathe life and ideas into you. Divide your fabrics into color families–try as I may, my fabric never stays this way. I'm convinced those pictures I've seen in magazines of quilters sewing studios have been seriously straightened for months, forever, before a camera was allowed inside. If you ever see my studio it will be a mess. Believe me if it's clean someone made me or I was really looking for something and in order to find it had to clean.

You need fabric in every color. Every single color. Include colors you really aren't fond of. My hardest color to work with is yellow. To me this is a very powerful color. It is sunshine and tropical looking. It's strong and too bright for me. But if we are to be artists we must work with every single color. We make quilts for others as well as ourselves and other people love yellow. I've included a yellow quilt in this book to prove I can work with yellow–the fabric was in my stash! Better news–I like the quilt and that's really what counts. I also learned how to work with yellow without it taking over. That's important to me, learning how to work with color. The only true way to do that is to make a quilt. And a bad quilt is better than a blanket any day.

A little note: you don't have to use all your stash in one quilt. If you have 3 yards and you only use one yard, maybe the next quilt will need the rest, maybe not. Your stash is where you store, supply, warehouse, put away, pack away, stowed away, deposit, lodge, and file your fabric. It's where you will look for magic. There to use and mix and blend and do wonderful things with. And please, never let someone tell you that you don't need a stash. There are times it's just nice to know it's there waiting for you to come into the room, rotary cutter in hand and an idea in your head. There are some that have a much larger stash than mine, but size isn't the key. If you can paint masterpieces the size you want from the stash you have then it's just the right size.

The yardages in this book are rounded up. My quilts were made from my stash and so should yours. In case you are going out to buy just enough for a project, the yardages in this book are what I used, plus a little, so you won't run out of fabric. Who knows, maybe you could start a stash.

I hope you understand I come from an art teaching background so the quality of the creativity is more important to me than to most. It's a very important part of quilting. Using your skills to sew is wonderful but using your mind as well is excellent.

What it takes to make a Crazy Project

Most books nowadays give great basic instruction and how to do quiltmaking from beginning to end. This little book is for those that already understand those methods. I will talk basics in some ways, but if you have your favorite method, use it. The patterns have actual templates available for ease as you may know. Templates made of metal can be used with a rotary cutter. These templates also have a "sandy" side that makes the fabric less slippery. Most of these patterns can be done in other ways. You can change the size of a pattern with little effort because of the magical methods of Mary Ellen Hopkins. If you understand and use her methods, this book will be another way to make interesting quilts with fast methods. If you don't know her methods and want to learn, try your local quilt shop. The owner and instructors there are people that could help. Even though I know Mary Ellen's methods, there are times the templates are easier. Any templates in the same shape should work. Be sure the seam allowance is included in your templates. Whenever you purchase template sets, understand they do not fit together until they are sewn. The 1/4" seam allowance that is added to the templates make them seem like they won't fit together, but they do. You just need a little blind faith sometimes.

Just a Little Crazy (Snowball)

Simple patterns are great. Beginners learn lots from patterns like this and Advanced Quiltmakers need to back up and relax. I have stopped working so hard and tried to let my fabrics work some overtime. This very traditional pattern can go crazy if we let it go.

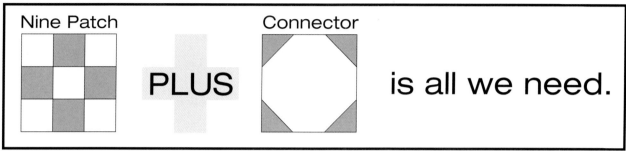

Diagram 6

1) Sew strips together to form 3 sets as shown (diag. 7). Iron towards dark fabric. Cut them apart using the same measurement as the width of your strips (mine was 1 5/8").

2) These will be sewn together to form a nine patch (diag. 8).

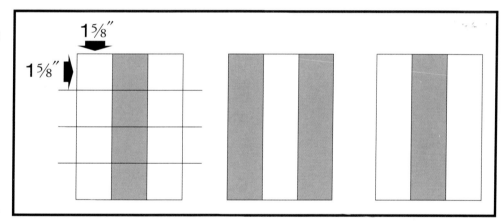

Diagram 7

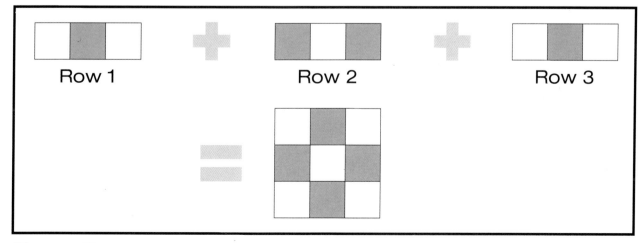

Diagram 8

3) Measure the nine patch, edge to edge. This is the measurement you will need to cut your squares for the connector blocks.

4) Cut print squares using the measurement of the nine patch. Some of these connectors will also be crazy so follow the instructions in "getting crazy" to make as many crazy connectors as you want. I made 8. Personally I like odd numbers when making things like this and planned on making only seven, but I got crazy and made an extra.

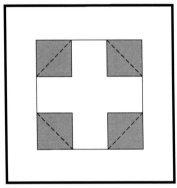

Diagram 9

5) Cut 4 squares of solid for each connector. These are cut the same size as your strips. (mine was 1 5/8"). Sew these squares to the corners of the connector blocks by sewing diagonally across. This can be done by swinging from square to square (diag. 9).

6) Cut away excess solid (not print or crazy). This is left to serve as a base and is the actual size needed. Sometimes the squares are a little off. Leaving the base will give you a true size to sew to the nine patches.

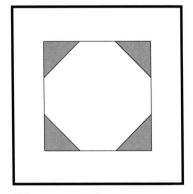

Diagram 10

7) Place your nine patches and connector blocks together alternating. Every once in a while throw in a crazy connector.

The plain solids looked awful until the gold stitching and beads were added. Beading is really fun when you do a small amount. This is done by hand and doesn't require much skill. Just pick up a bead on your needle and sew it down. I use a "sharp" needle and nymo thread. You can find beads in bead stores, quilt shops, and cross-stitch shops. Once you have put on a few beads it will change your outlook on those beaded dresses. Beads add such a spark to the otherwise "flat" look of a quilt. If you don't know any fancy stitches and don't have any on your machine, beads are the way to go. This hand work can be done with the family all around.

Twisted Star (Party Hats)

Because I like the word "twisted" and it is more modern than just "crazy," this pattern had to be included in the fun. Any pattern that goes together in a nine patch configuration is a favorite of mine (diag. 19). The blocks are based on the nine patch, a very simple block of 9 squares. This block can change completely by adding triangles. In fact a nine patch is like magic. By adding extra shapes the changes can go on forever. In Twisted Star we just add 2 triangles (diag. 20). The templates give you two sizes to choose from so you can make either size.

Diagram 11

The method of measurement-then-sew gives you a better chance of the pattern pieces fitting. You make a unit that has the most parts and make the others fit to that unit. This is a good example.

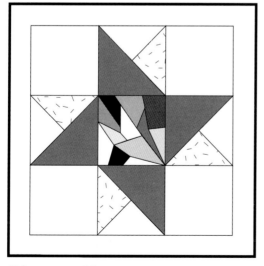

Diagram 12

Yardage: 1 1/2 yards background, 1/4 yard teal green, 1/4 yard hot pink, 1 yard large print (enough for border), scraps for crazy.

1) Sew triangle units together.
You need 4 per block. Press.

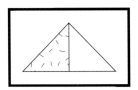

Diagram 13

2) Sew triangle units to larger
triangle. Notice where your
straight grain is going.

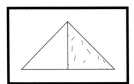

Diagram 14

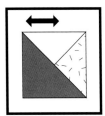

Diagram 15

This unit can get a little out of whack if bias is running
around. On your smaller triangles be sure the straight of
grain is on the short side (diag. 23).
This will make the block straighter.

Diagram 16

If the bias is on the outside edge you'll get a dip in the block that simply
can't be fixed. Once you have this unit sewn, measure the square. This
measurement is the size you will need for the crazy center as well as the
corner blocks. Make the crazy centers following the instructions in the
section "getting crazy." Then trim your finished crazy the size of your measurement.

For some extra excitement I added beads to this quilt. There are some in
the border as well. Also, this crazy has velvets & cottons in it, together. It
gives a very different look. If you plan to wash your quilt be sure to use
washable velvets.

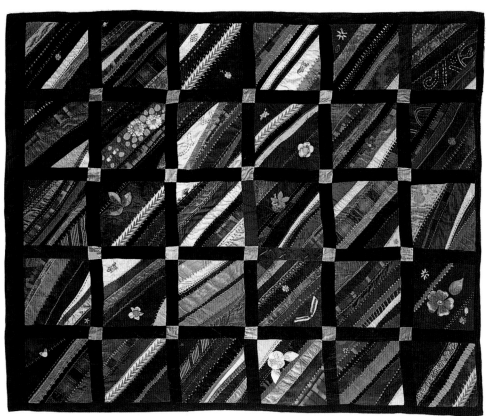

1950's Crazy Quilt from my Godmother Min McElvy

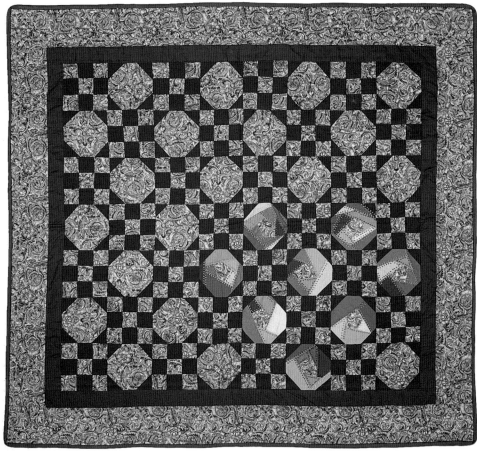

Just A Little Crazy

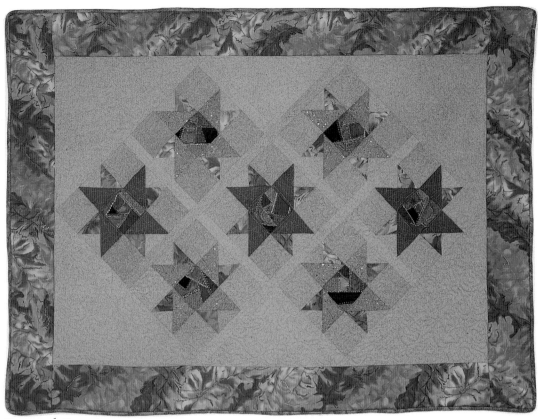

Twisted Star (cover)

Crazy Day and Night

Crazy Stars

Lazy Crazy Days of Summer

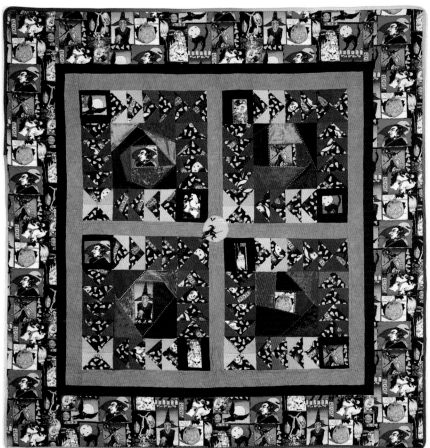

I'm Crazy About Halloween (back cover)

Cabin Fever Crazy (Log Cabin)

This is a favorite pattern of mine. It is very old and traditional but this makes it makeable and it was great making it crazy. The suede-look fabrics from Cherrywood were in my stash. These fabrics actually told me to buy them. They are so beautiful it's very difficult to ignore them screaming at you. So of course I bought them with the wish to someday sew with them. It's great the way people always want to touch it, they think the crazy is suede. It drives them crazy!

Diagram 17

The project doesn't need much, a few 1/2 yard pieces for your blocks and about 1 yard for the set in triangles. There are two reds, two greens and four blacks in my blocks.

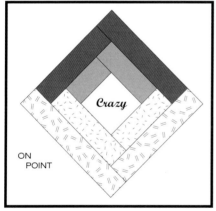

Diagram 18

*If you have never made a log cabin before you will find instructions in most basic books. If you don't understand my directions try Eleanor Burns' Quilt in a Day Log Cabin Book. You can use any size strips. I like my "logs" smaller than 2 1/2" like Eleanor uses. This size is good for a large quilt but I like the look of smaller strips.

How to:

1) Pick a number or size you want your centers to be. This will be your very own size. I picked 4 1/2" because it is the width of the ruler I had. Using this size for your base, follow the instructions in "getting crazy" for your centers. Trim your base fabric to 4 1/2" or your size when finished.

2) Pick the width you want your strips to be. I picked 1 3/4". Cut 2 strips of the first two blacks, 4 strips of the second two blacks, 3 of the first red and green and 5 of the second red and green (the "first" meaning from the center out).

3) Take your first blacks and sew it to your crazy centers.

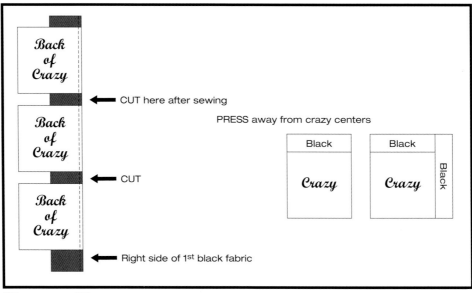

Diagram 19

4) Take another of your first black strips and sew it to the other side of your crazy centers (diag. 14). My quilt has 7 green blocks and 6 red blocks. Do this to all your blocks at the same time. Cut a part and press away from centers.

Diagram 20

5) Take a first red strip and sew it to 6 of the blocks. Take a green strip and sew to 7 of the blocks. Sewing in a clockwise motion, sew another red and green strip to complete the "round." Do another "round" of black and red or green to complete the blocks (diag. 15).

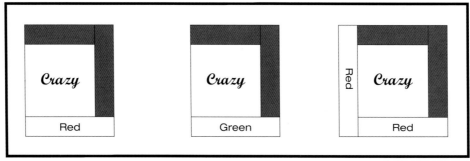

Diagram 21

The setting for this quilt is on point. Just turn the block a quarter turn and the block changes. This also gives you a larger block because the measurement from A to B is greater than C to B (diag. 16).

This quilt could be made larger by adding blank squares between the log cabins. I like the block to block setting because the logs come together and form a fake sashing.

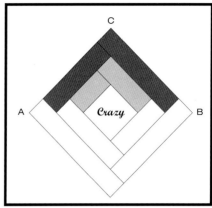

Diagram 22

To get the measurement for the set-in triangles, measure your block from point A to B, and add 3". Cut 2 squares this size and cut into 4 triangles per edges and outside 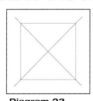 triangles (diag. 17). This will give you four tri-square. The straight of grain will be on the long since that is where you want it it's perfect. The edge of your quilt needs to always be straight as possible. These triangles are pieced to your blocks, like blocks but will be larger. You can always cut away, but never able to add more if it's too small.

Diagram 23

The corner triangles need to have the straight of grain on the short sides. I usually cut a square about 2" bigger than my block, measures from point C to B (diag. 16). Then cut in half. The extra that this method gives allows the blocks to float (diag. 18). If you want extra on the edges before your border, it's there. Sometimes the blocks don't line up as nicely as planned and this extra float will let your eye miss this. Usually I trim to about 1" and sew the borders.

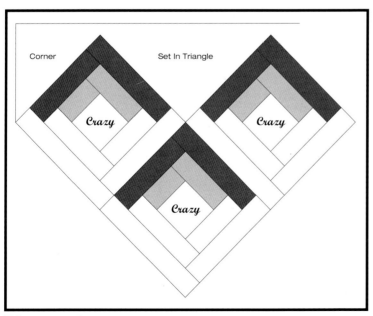

Diagram 24

Crazy Day and Night (Night and Noon)

This pattern is a favorite of my husbands.' The blocks go well with almost every fabric. I pulled some of my favorites for this quilt. I think it's a great quilt to dedicate to Michael because I know I drove him crazy day and night for the entire 16 years we were married.

The print was pulled first, then the solids that work well with the print. The gold thread adds a spark to the centers.

Yardages: 1/2 yard of print
1/4 yard each of solids (3).
1 1/2 yard of black
1/2 yard solid for border
Scraps for crazy

Diagram 25

How to:

1) Make the crazy centers following instructions in "getting crazy." The pattern is easier to make using the templates. This means your base needs to be 6 1/2" and trimmed to size later.

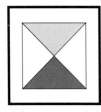

Diagram 26

2) Make 4 of this unit for each block. Watch the color location.

3) Make 4 of this unit for each block. This unit, the above unit and the crazy center all should be the same size. Trim your center to this size.

Diagram 27

4) Once all the units are constructed, sew the rows together like a nine patch. Three rows of 3 units.

Diagram 28

Notice the setting on this quilt. One night I made these blocks and stopped. When I returned to them I wasn't in the mood to do anymore. I love putting blocks on point so using a felt board I started putting these blocks on the board in any way I could think of without making any more blocks. (You could make more, it's a challenge of lazy vs intellectualize. I'm so lazy sometimes I would rather just think of an easier way not to make any more blocks.) That's how this setting came to be. I also used similar settings for 2 of the other quilts.

Something again about diagonal sets, they are for the lazy. A few blocks go much farther set this way. People often don't recognize a block that is turned, either (diag. 28).

Also, let me say how rarely quilts go the way I plan. Sometimes I run out of a color–sometimes like in this quilt it actually fell behind something, got buried and lost until after I had cut and used something close enough. This doesn't bother me. If it bothers you then be sure to buy extra fabric. My friend, Ann Boyce, says I was Amish in another life because I always manage at least one mistake in my quilts. I'm not trying to make them, they just happen. My quilts will be easily spotted after I'm gone because they are full of character and were made by a character. For some reason it's not hard for me to make mistakes in my quilts. In the beginning it was hard to leave them alone, now, if the pieces fit the mistake stays. Mistakes are in the eyes of the beholder.

Crazy Stars (Aunt Eliza's Star)

This is the quilt that started the insanity. If you are going to go crazy only once, use some fabrics you never used before. Lame' isn't easy to work with unless you iron some interfacing to it. They will handle much better and actually let you enjoy them.

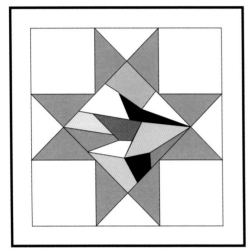

Diagram 29

Yardages: 1 yard print, 3/4 yard background, 1/2 yard sash, fatquarters of lame' for centers.

How to:

1) This block lends itself to a large center so the crazy is very big. My center was 6". Follow the "getting crazy" instructions to make your crazy centers.

2) Using templates or your own method, cut triangles from print. Cut 8 for each block (diag. 30).

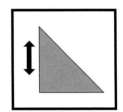

Diagram 30

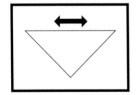

Diagram 31

Also cut 4 for each block from background fabric (diag. 31).

3) Cut squares from background fabric, 4 for each block.

4) Sew triangles to squares. Make 2 of these for each block (diag. 32).

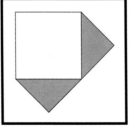

Diagram 32

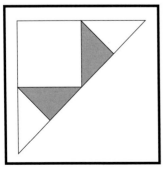

Diagram 33

5) Sew triangles to squares. Make 2 of these for each block (diag. 33).

6) Sew units made in #4 to crazy center. One on each opposite side (diag. 34).

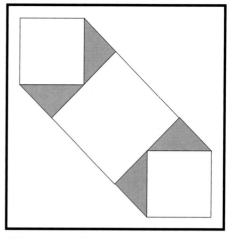

Diagram 34

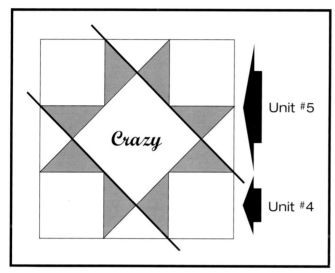

Unit #5

Unit #4

Crazy

Diagram 35

7) Sew units made in #5 to the #6 units (diag. 35).

Because this quilt has so much going on it is set with a plain traditional straight set with sashing.

Do not be afraid to stop. There is so much going on within these blocks if a special setting or anything extra was added, it could take away from the look. Sometimes people do go crazy. Take the Christmas season for example. There is a very fine line between really gorgeous and truly tacky. The same is true in quiltmaking. Sometimes it is better to stop adding more lights and brights. Let the fabric shine, but don't go blind.

This came true the year there seemed to be a competition between a neighbor and myself and lots of white Christmas lights. First I loaded my bushes with these tiny lights and had white candle lights in my windows. He did the same but added lights to his porch. So I added them to my porch and the trees. When he finally climbed on the roof and outlined his house I realized just how tacky his house looked. So I stopped turning on my lights until a few had been taken off. You can lose and still win the game. And I remember how cold it was in January when those lights were taken out of the bushes. But at least I wasn't on the roof.

Lazy Crazy Days of Summer with a Crazy Loon Border (SawTooth Star with a Flying Geese Border)

The yellow fabric that didn't take over, but added sunshine to my summer.

The method shown for sewing this block is magical. You will need great faith to follow. If you just can't bear to follow, use the templates.

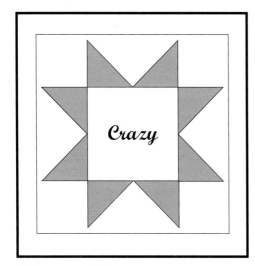

Diagram 36

Yardages: 1 yard print, 2 yards background, scraps for crazy centers.

How to:
1) Crazy centers–pick a number or size you would like your crazy centers to be. (Mine were made 6" because that's the width of my ruler.) Follow the instructions in "getting crazy."

2) This unit is the loon border unit as well as the star unit.

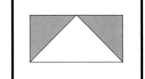

Diagram 37

Because math eludes me this method requires very little math. This unit needs to be the same size as the crazy center. Mine is 6" and to make this even easier this unit will be 3" wide.

Cut a rectangle 6" X 3", 4 are needed for each block.
Cut 2 squares 3" for each of the rectangles.

Diagram 38

Fold the squares in half and finger press them. This will give you a guide to sew along (diag. 38). Put a square in the corner of the rectangle and sew diagonally across the square (diag. 39).

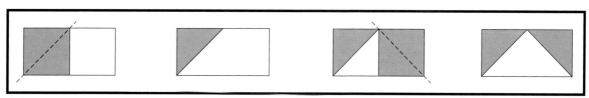

Diagram 39

Press the bottom half back to form a triangle. The extra fabric can be cut away. I cut the extra part of the square. The rectangle was cut the exact size needed to be there for a base. That little extra will not effect the block. Put another square on the rectangle and sew the same way. This will give you the loon unit. You should have some extra up at the top–an overlap. This is your 1/4" seam allowance. If it's not there you will loose the point. Sometimes I think about writing a book called, "What's the Point?" Because I loose points from time to time. But I learned a long time ago that my next quilt will be better. I will never finish if I am always worried about every point.

3) The corner squares are the same size as the width of your units = 3".

4) Sew the blocks together using the 3 rows of 3 units–a nine patch.

You have now made a block the way I really make blocks, making up measurements as I go. As for the settings used for this quilt, I finished the blocks late one night with no desire to make more. These blocks didn't seem to be the same size either. So I added a small strip in between them (sashing). This gave a floating effect that I have grown to love because it hides the fact that they aren't the same size. This is a great idea for group quilts. By adding the sash it will give each quilter a feeling of perfect.

Mathwise this border is a miracle, nothing less.

It just fit. Really, I didn't plan it at all. There were extra loon units and some extra crazy centers. I sewed some, measured, and they fit. Simply a miracle!

I'm Crazy about Halloween

A while ago I was lucky enough to meet two outstanding young people. As luck would have it these two became good friends of mine. Over the years we have enjoyed many fine meals, lots of fun and nights filled with laughter but most of all they have shared some of their great fabrics with me. These two designers are the brat pack from Alexander Henry fabrics, Phillip & Nicole DeLeon. When you see these two they are always nice, polite and very polished. Under all that they are nicer, more polite and just plain perfect. They need to be thanked for letting me make quilts for them. A few years ago Philip sent me fabrics and that started my brain going crazy. This quilt can be done with any seasonal print–but try to use one of theirs.

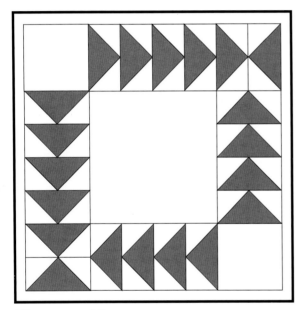

Diagram 40

The same quilt would look great in Christmas prints and even some tropical prints. The large area in the center lends itself to a lot of creativeness.

Because I always design backwards I really am having a hard time explaining this pattern. Not because it's hard, but because I'm silly. (I really didn't think while doing it.) So this is written the way I actually designed the quilt.

Diagram 41

1) The flying geese unit is the beginning. This unit has 2 small triangles on either side of a larger triangle. We don't want the center too large so we must watch the size we choose for the geese unit. The center should be about 8". The geese will need to be about 2" each. (Easy measurements are the only way) So, the unit is made just like the one in "Lazy Crazy Days of Summer," just the measurements are different. The rectangle will be 4 1/2", the squares 2 1/2". Following the directions on #2 in "Lazy Day" make 20 units for each of the 4 blocks.

2) Sew 4 of these units together to form a side. Measure the side. This will be the size you will need to make the crazy center. Even if your sizes are smaller or larger than you think, this is the measurement that is important. The reason for this is that every person isn't perfect. In fact, no one is perfect. We all try to sew an exact 1/4" seam, but it doesn't always happen. This way, no matter what, the center will fit because it's the same size as the geese unit.

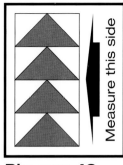

Diagram 42

Plus, there really is no math involved. Some people are into math. That's fine. I'm not and, trust me, my bank can tell you adding and subtracting is a challenge for me, so there is no sense doing something I hate while trying to do something I love. This method works.

3) Sew the crazy center following the instructions in "getting crazy." Trim to the size needed for your centers. Mine was 8 1/2." (With lots of heavy material like velvets, you may want a larger seam allowance.)

4) Sew the geese units to the sides of the crazy center (diag. 43).

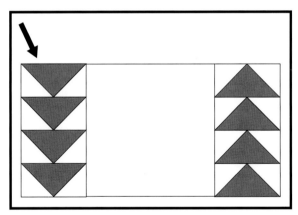

Diagram 43

5) Because the fabric that I was given is really great looking, I made something crooked in the corners. You have no idea how hard it is to try and sew something crooked. But the idea of Halloween and crooked got to me and I guess I lost it. Two of the corners can be done, all four can be done this way or none. I cut out the pictures from the fabric and sewed different width fabric strips to the side thinking this would look something like crooked (diag. 44). Then I trimmed to the size needed (4 1/2"). Sew these units to one end of the geese units (diag. 45).

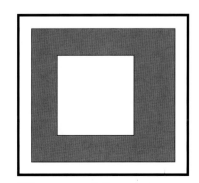

Diagram 44

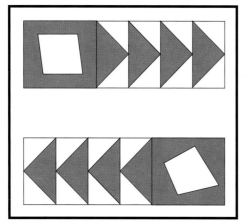

Diagram 45

6) Take two geese units and sew them to-gether with tips touching (diag. 46).

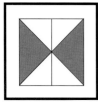

Diagram 46

7) Sew this unit to the other end of the top & bottom units (diag. 47).

I made 4 of the ground solid fab-shades of yellow to fabric was a hand-

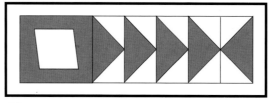

Diagram 47

blocks. The back-rics were different orange/red. The dyed batch from

Cherrywood. They had 1/4 yard pieces of about 8 colors. Use as many or as few as you want. These blocks were too busy to put side-by-side so I put a sashing of 2 1/2" in orange and a border in black 1 1/2" and a large 4 1/2" border in the print. I used the large print for the centers of my crazy. My crazy was made with velvets. The geese units were made with a candy corn print.

Yardage: 1/4 yard each of about 8 different yellow or orange/red solids
            1 1/2 yards candy corn
            1 yard orange (sashing)
            3/4 yard black (border & corners)
            1 Yard print (large border & centers)

Templates

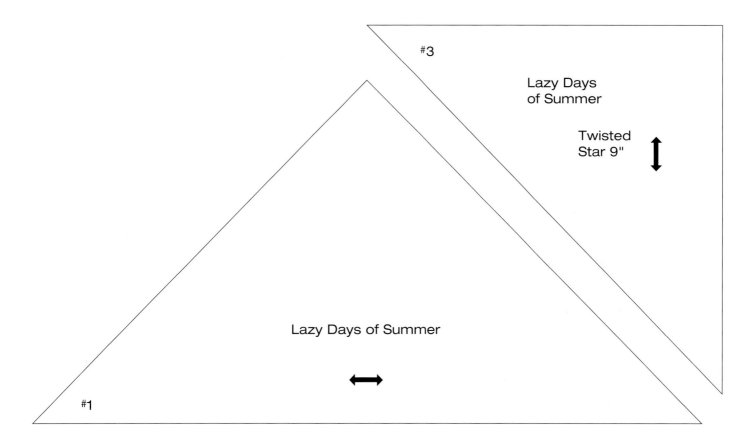

#3

Lazy Days
of Summer

Twisted
Star 9"

Lazy Days of Summer

#1

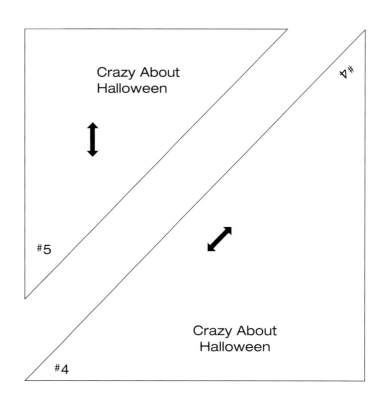

Twisted Star 9"

Lazy Days of Summer

#9

Crazy About
Halloween

#4

#5

Crazy About
Halloween

#4

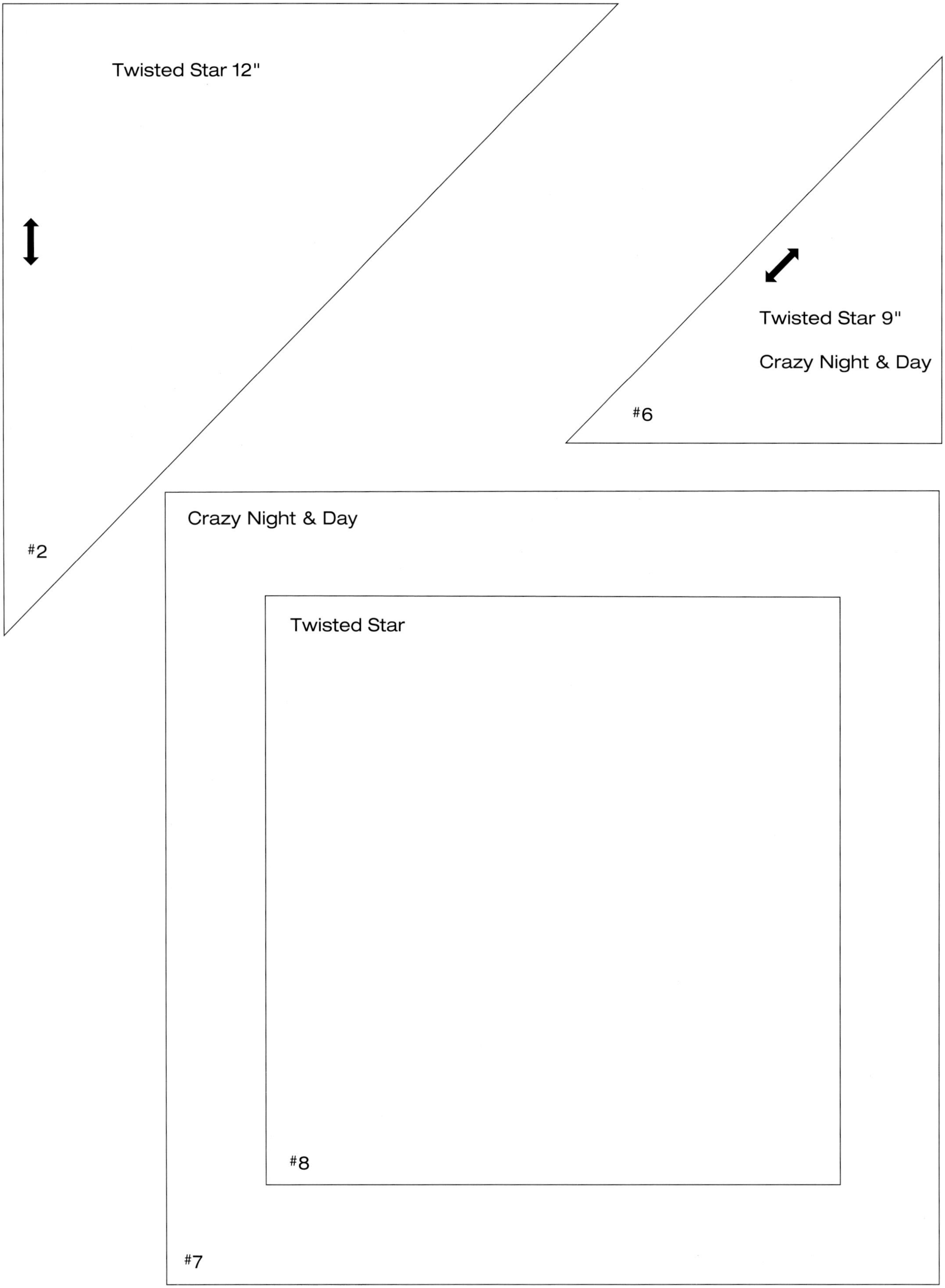

Twisted Star 12"

↕

#2

↗

Twisted Star 9"

Crazy Night & Day

#6

Crazy Night & Day

Twisted Star

#8

#7

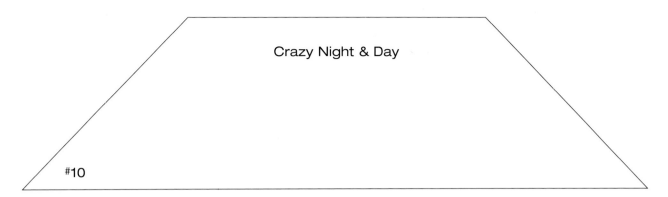

Crazy Night & Day

#10

Footnote

Now that I have written a book and proved to myself that it can be done I am sadden to think the crazy will end for me. The greatest part of teaching has always been watching my students go beyond my ideas. I truly hope you will show me up on this crazy stuff and take it farther. And may the crazy in each of us take us far.

About The Author

Charlotte comes from a military family that traveled around during her childhood. She was born in Montgomery, Alabama and has lived in Mississippi, Georgia, New Mexico and Virginia.

She graduated from Huntingdon College in Montgomery with an art major, speech and drama minor with secondary education.

While shopping with her mother in 1977, they wondered into a quilt store and changed her life. The art form of quiltmaking has become not only a hobby but her job. In 1981 she opened Quilt Works in Virginia Beach.

After all these years of quiltmaking, teaching quilting and now writing a book on quilting, she still finds quilting exciting.

Charlotte does classes and workshops for quilt guilds and shops.